OUR AMAZING WORLD

ANTS

Kay de Silva

Aurora

Contents

An ant on a blade of grass.

ANTS

Ants are insects that are close relatives of wasps and bees. They evolved from their wasp-like ancestors 130 million years ago. This makes them as old as dinosaurs.

An ant displaying its awesome strength.

ANATOMY

Ants are *invertebrates* or creatures that have no backbones. They have *exoskeletons* or external skeletons that make them strong and flexible.

They also have large heads, powerful jaws, and elbowed *antennae*. Ants are often mistaken for termites. Unlike termites, however, ants have slender waists between their *abdomens* and *thoraxes*.

Ants are among the world's strongest creatures in relation to their size. They also work together in small and large groups to move heavy objects. Most ants can carry 20 times their body weight. If you were as strong as an ant, you'd be able to lift a small car.

Black Ants returning to their underground nest in the desert.

HABITAT

Ants are tough creatures and can be found on every continent of the world except Antarctica. Abundant in tropical forests, they may make up half of all insects living in some of these areas.

For every human being there are about one million ants. The total weight of all the ants in the world equals the weight of the entire human race.

SENSES & COMMUNICATION

Most ant *species* or types have poor eyesight. Some ants, such as *Driver Ants*, are completely blind.

Ants also don't have ears. They use their feet to *hear* by feeling vibrations in the ground. The two antennae or feelers attached to their heads help detect chemicals, air currents, and vibrations.

When it comes to communication, these insects never disagree on what they have to do. Instead, they follow their own in-built rules and signals in the form of touch, vibrations, and chemical smells and get the job done.

Ants touch antenna to communicate and "kiss" to pass food.

MOVEMENT

Unlike their wasp-like ancestors, only some ants have wings. Most ants travel by walking. Some types of ants, such as *Jerdon's Jumping Ants*, can leap.

There are also species of wingless ants that can glide. These ants can control the direction of their descent when free falling. Such ants that live in the canopies of tropical rain forests glide to return to their home tree trunk when they fall off of branches. This helps them avoid the dangers of the forest floor and of losing their way.

Building an ant bridge facilitates movement.

ANTS IN WATER

Ants don't have lungs or gills. They breathe through *spiracles* or small holes found around their bodies. *Oxygen* enters their bodies through these holes, and *carbon dioxide* exits through them.

A species of ants found in mangrove swamps in Australia can live in underwater nests. They use trapped pockets of air in these nests to breathe.

Only a few ant species can swim. Most ants can survive underwater for about 24 hours. When ants drown in a flood, they may appear dead. If the water *evaporates* and there is enough oxygen flowing through their spiracles, they can miraculously come back to life.

Some ant species build chains to bridge gaps over water. Others form floating rafts that help survive floods and allow ants to colonise islands.

An ant quenching its thirst.

DIET

Ants typically feed on nectar, seeds, or insects. Some species have more unusual diets. For instance, *Army Ants* may prey on reptiles, birds, or even small mammals.

When *foraging* or looking for food, ants leave a *pheromone* or scent trail so they know where they've been. These trails are also used to alert other ants to danger or lead them to a promising food source.

Sharing food enables some ants to look after the nest while others forage for food. Ants often carry crumbs, leaves, and dead insects in their jaws to share with the colony.

Ants also have two stomachs. One stomach holds food for them, and the second holds food for others. When you see ants *kissing*, they are actually feeding each other from their *social stomachs* or *crops*.

Ants feasting on a bee.

COLONIES

Ants are social insects, which mean they live in large groups or *colonies*. Colonies have several rooms connected by tunnels. Depending on the species, each colony may consist of millions of ants.

Much like human societies, in ant colonies labor is divided, and each ant must do a specific task. They also work together to solve problems and support the group.

Colonies of ants sometimes merge to create super colonies that house multiple queens. The largest super colony ever discovered is found in Europe. It is made up of millions of nests and billions of *Argentinian Ants*. This super colony stretches across 3,750 miles (6,000 kilometers), which is the distance from London to Washington DC.

Worker ants dragging vegetation to the colony.

QUEENS & DRONES

An ant colony is headed by a *queen*. Depending on the species, a colony may have one or many queens. Her role is to ensure the survival of the colony by producing young ants, which are known as a *brood*. A queen is called a *princess* before she mates.

A male ant is called a *drone*. A Drone doesn't do any work in the colony. Its only role is to mate with the princess.

Both princesses and drones have wings. A princess sheds her wings after mating and starting a new nest. She is then known as a queen and spends her life laying eggs.

A drone lives a few weeks and dies after it mates. A queen can live as long as 30 years, the longest of all insects. During her lifetime she can have millions of *offspring*. When the queen of the colony dies, she's rarely replaced. Without her the colony can survive only a few months.

A Carpenter Ant drone resting on a leaf.

Red Ant Queen and Workers.

WORKERS

As only queens can produce young, other wingless female ants in the colony take on the roles of *workers* or *soldiers*.

Workers are also known as *minor workers* and are the most common ants found in a colony. They are the smallest ants that do the most work. They care for the queen and offspring, forage for food, maintain and expand the nest, and defend the colony.

Foraging workers can travel up to 700 feet (200 meters) from their nests. They find their way back to their colonies by following scent trails left by other ants.

A soldier ant is larger than a worker.

SOLDIERS

Soldier ants are present among some ant species. Soldiers are also known as *major workers* or *big heads*.

These female ants are larger and stronger than worker ants. They protect the queen and colony from large predators, gather food or hunt prey, and attack enemy colonies in search of food and nesting space. They also use their strength and *mandibles* or large jaws to cut and carry large objects.

NESTS

Colonies are typically housed in structured nest communities. These nests may be located underground, in mounds above the ground, or in trees. *Carpenter Ants* nest in wood and may be destructive to buildings.

Ants carefully select their nesting sites. The material used for construction includes soil and plant matter. They are quick to abandon their nests at the first sign of a threat.

Army Ants defy the norm and do not build permanent nests. Instead they sometimes prefer *nomadism* or moving from place to place. When these ants rest between hunting raids, they build *temporary* nests, using their bodies by holding each other together. This nest is known as a *bivouac*.

A bivouac may be inside a hollow log or out in the open hanging from a tree limb. Thousands of workers link their legs and mandibles and build an eclipsed hammock for the queen. Sometimes immature ants rest inside the hammock as well.

Ants tending the brood chamber.

LIFE CYCLE

All ants go through a similar process to reach adulthood. This is known as their life cycle and is a form of *metamorphosis*, which is the same process a caterpillar uses to change into a butterfly. Ants' life cycles can take from a few weeks to a year to complete.

The *nuptial flight* is the first stage of the life cycle. This is when princesses and drones take to the sky to mate. After mating, the drone dies, and the princess becomes a queen and is ready to start her own colony. She will find a place to nest and lay her first eggs.

The eggs will turn into *larvae* and are similar to maggots. They, however, have no eyes or major organs and just wiggle and open their mouths. The queen and worker ants help feed them.

Most larvae grow into worker ants. Well-fed larvae grow up to become winged princesses. Fully grown larvae will begin to take the form of adult ants. Most species will spin a silk *cocoon* around themselves. This stage is known as the *pupa*.

In time pale yellow ants emerge. At these early stages the ants are known as *nantics* or *minims*. They quickly darken as their exoskeletons darken and grow strong as they feed.

Newly hatched ants, known as callows, emerging from pupa.

A Red Fire Ant duel.

ENEMIES & SLAVES

Ants' worst enemies are other ants. Even within the same species, ants treat those from different colonies as rivals. When ants fight, it's usually to the death. They use their mandibles to hold the legs or antennae of opponents, while nest mates tear victims apart.

Some ant species make slaves out of other ant species. This can happen in two ways. A queen ant may pay a visit to another colony and kill the resident queen. She'll take over the nest and use the workers to bring up her own eggs.

Slave making can also happen when workers or soldiers invade and conquer another colony. The winners may steal these nests off their eggs, larvae, or pupae. When the young are fully grown, and if they are not eaten first, they become slaves within the invaders' colony.

Ants harvesting aphids.

FARMING

Much like humans, ants are great farmers. Many ants have developed special bonds with invertebrates and plants for *mutual benefit*. A common practice is *farming* or *herding sap feeding* insects. These include aphids, mealy bugs, and scale bugs.

Aphids suck sap from plants and excrete waste known as *honeydew*. Ants thrive on this sugar-rich nectar. Hungry ants *milk* droplets of honeydew by stroking aphids' backs with their antennae.

In turn the aphid-herding ants make sure their cattle are healthy, well fed, and safe. They do this by moving the aphids to areas on plants with the best sap. The ants also protect these insects from predators and parasites. When it rains, the ants move them to sheltered places, sometimes into their own nests.

ARMY ANTS

Army Ants are also known as *Driver Ants*, *Legionary Ants*, and *Visiting Ants*. They are found in Africa and South America. A colony of Army Ants consists of about 700,000 ants.

Known for their nomadic lifestyle, Army Ants march in the thousands. Some species migrate in a line, while others move in a fan-shaped wave. Soldiers position themselves on the sides of the column to defend the queen. Workers carry immature ants.

They rest in a bivouac for a few weeks. Once the queen comes out of her resting place, the colony begins their onward march.

Army Ants are fierce group *predators* with amazing digestive systems that dissolve their prey with ease. On the move, workers kill every living creature in their wake and gather all the food they can. Animals who hear the sound of marching ants rush to get out of their way.

A trail of Army Ants on a deadly mission.

HARVESTER ANTS

Different species of *Harvester Ants* are found around the world. They get their name because of their habit of using their pincers to cut grass and build large mounds.

The *Maricopa Harvester Ant* is the most venomous insect on the planet. Its sting is as powerful as 12 honey bees.

Their favourite food is seeds, which they gather from different grasses. Workers collect seeds from as far as 35 miles (56 kilometers) from their nests. Soldiers use their mandibles to crack open hard seeds. The ants grind seeds into a *bread*, which is placed in storage areas in their nests called *granaries*. They also eat other insects and spiders.

A few *Horned Lizard* species prey only on Harvester Ants. They have adapted ways to survive ant stings and attacks. In areas where Harvester Ants are being invaded by Argentine Ants, Horned Lizards have become an *endangered* species.

Portrait of a Harvester Ant.

LEAF CUTTER ANTS

Leaf Cutter Ants or *Parasol Ants* are found in the tropical forests of Central and South America and in some southern parts of the United States. They are known as the farmers of the insect world because they grow their own food.

Leaf Cutter Ants travel long distances to find better *foliage* or leaves. They move in a single line, clearing everything in the way. They often leave visible trails through the forest floor. A colony of these ants can strip a full-grown tree of its leaves in one day. This equals as much as a full-grown cow can consume in the same amount of time.

Soldiers use their sharp mandibles to cut through thicker plants. Minor workers carry the clippings on their backs to their underground nests. They don't eat the leaves. Instead, they chew the leaves into a pulp and store it in the burrow. The chunks of pulp are mixed ant waste and fungus spores. Strands of fungus grow on the composting pile.

The colony feasts on the fungus, which also provides the topsoil with nourishment for plants. These ants are the best recyclers on the planet.

A busy colony of Leaf Cutter Ants.

TRAP JAW ANTS

Trap Jaw Ants are originally from South America. They get their name from their mandibles, which protrude from their heads and shut horizontally. These jaws are not just for decoration. These ants have the fastest bite on the planet.

Their mandibles can exert as much force as 300 times their weight, which, coupled with speed, makes these ants formidable predators. Because their mandibles move at 140 mph (miles per hour), you cannot see these ants close their jaws. It happens 2,300 times faster than you blink your eyes.

These ants also use their mandibles against predators. Known as *bouncer defence*, the ants slam their mandibles against their targets to injure them or bounce them away. This could also catapult an ant up to 15 inches (12.7 centimeters) away. The distance, translated to a 5-foot-6-inch (1.68 meter) tall athlete, equals 132 feet (40 meters), which is over 4 times the current Olympic record.

Alternatively, Trap Jaw Ants may use *escape* jumps to flee predators and escape difficult *terrain*. They do this by snapping their jaws against the ground. This launches them up to 3 inches (7.6 centimeters) into the air. For the same athlete, that equals 44 feet (13.4 meters) up. The current world high jump record is just over 8 feet (2.4 meters).

A close-up of a Trap Jaw Ant.

WEAVER ANTS

Weaver Ants or *Tailor Ants* are found in Australia and Southeast Asia. They are frequently found in forest trees and are best known for their fascinating nest construction. These nests consist of living leaves joined in a ball using specially produced silk.

To do this, a team of ants link their legs and create strong chains to bridge a gap between two leaves. A second team holds the tent-like position together. A third team of ants holds Weaver Ant larvae in their mandibles. Gently squeezing these little tubes of glue creates a mat of silk between the leaves. In this way they create a ball of leaves, which becomes their home.

These highly *territorial* ants defend their territories against intruders. When these ants bite, they squirt *formic acid* into the wound, making it extremely painful. Birds pick up these ants in their beaks and place them in their feathers to kill mites living there. Farmers in China have used Weaver Ants to protect their fruit orchards from agricultural pests as far back as 304 AD.

Weaver Ants repairing their nest in the Australian Outback.

A team of ants constructing a bridge at sunset.

LIVING IN HARMONY

Every year ants move about 50 tons (45 tonnes) of solid earth in a single square mile (1.6 square kilometers), which makes ants more prolific soil turners than earthworms. Unfortunately, despite this and other contributions to our environment, most people regard ants as pests.

Next time you see a trail of ants, stop for a moment and observe. Notice their team work, perseverance, and environmental harmony. Ants have a lot to teach us about how we can make our planet a better place.

OUR AMAZING WORLD

COLLECT THEM ALL

WWW.OURAMAZINGWORLDBOOKS.COM

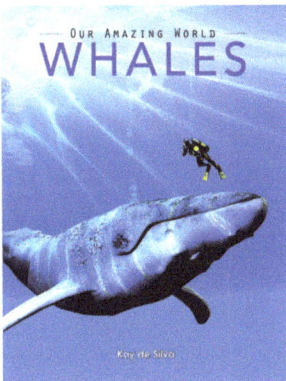

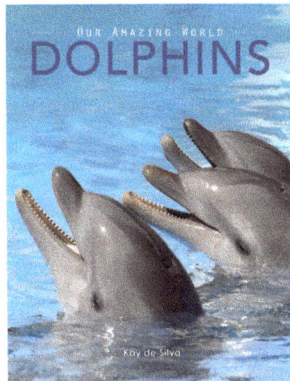

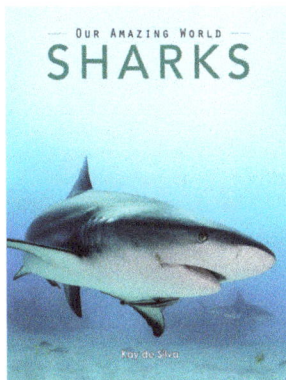

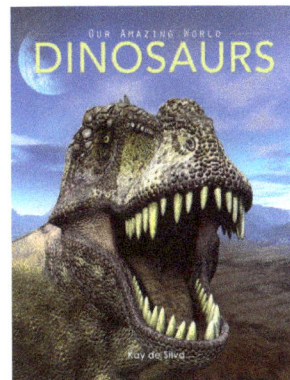

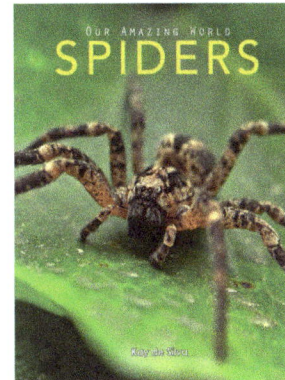

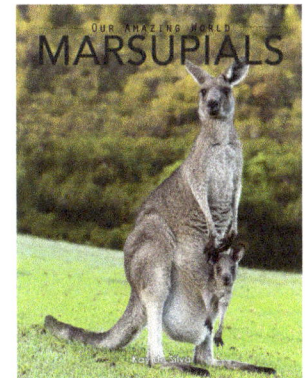

OUR AMAZING WORLD
WHALES
Kay de Silva

OUR AMAZING WORLD
DOLPHINS
Kay de Silva

OUR AMAZING WORLD
SEA TURTLES
Kay de Silva

OUR AMAZING WORLD
PENGUINS
Kay de Silva

OUR AMAZING WORLD
SHARKS
Kay de Silva

OUR AMAZING WORLD
DINOSAURS
Kay de Silva

OUR AMAZING WORLD
SPIDERS
Kay de Silva

OUR AMAZING WORLD
SNAKES
Kay de Silva

OUR AMAZING WORLD
TIGERS
Kay de Silva

OUR AMAZING WORLD
BEARS
Kay de Silva

OUR AMAZING WORLD
HORSES
Kay de Silva

OUR AMAZING WORLD
MARSUPIALS
Kay de Silva

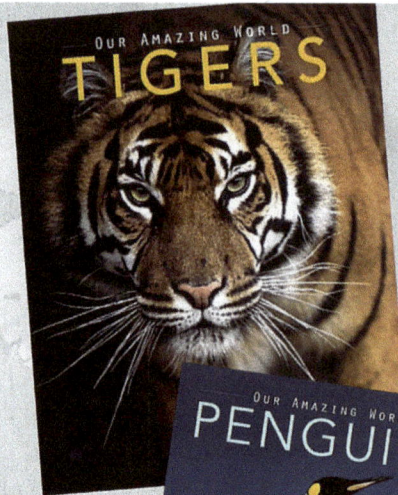

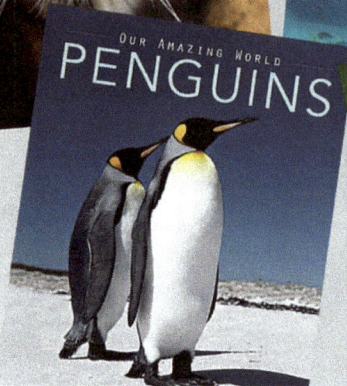

Aurora
An imprint of CKTY Publishing Solutions

ouramazingworldbooks.com

Text copyright © Kay de Silva, 2016
The moral right of the author has been asserted

ISBN 978-0-9946009-4-3

shutterstock.com

www.ingramcontent.com/pod-product-compliance
Lightning Source LLC
LaVergne TN
LVHW070834080426

835508LV00027B/3443